How to Find a Fox

Written by
KATE GARDNER

Photographs by
OSSI SAARINEN

RP|KIDS
PHILADELPHIA

For Julia, Nora, Easton, Maeve, Greyson, and Margaux:
may you all be lucky enough to find a fox one day. —K.G.

For Tran Le: whose love of all cute animals
motivates me to take more photos. —O.S.

Other animals featured: Egyptian geese, red squirrel,
American mink, and Canada goose gosling
Other animal tracks featured: red squirrel and mountain hare

Running Press Kids
Hachette Book Group
1290 Avenue of the Americas, New York, NY 10104
www.runningpress.com/rpkids
@RP_Kids

Printed in China

First Edition: September 2021

Published by Running Press Kids, an imprint of Perseus Books, LLC,
a subsidiary of Hachette Book Group, Inc. The Running Press Kids name and logo
is a trademark of the Hachette Book Group.

The Hachette Speakers Bureau provides a wide range of authors for speaking events.
To find out more, go to www.hachettespeakersbureau.com or call (866) 376-6591

The publisher is not responsible for websites (or their content)
that are not owned by the publisher.

Print book cover and interior design by Frances J. Soo Ping Chow

Library of Congress Control Number: 2020940916

ISBNs: 9780762471355 (hardcover), 9780762471348 (ebook),
9780762471478 (ebook), 9780762471485 (ebook)

1010

10 9 8 7 6 5 4 3 2 1

If you want to find a fox,
you can look in the forest . . .

or the meadow,

or even the city.

While foxes probably prefer their natural woodland home, they are very adaptable and can make do just about anywhere, including back-yards and back streets of suburbs and cities. There, human food waste is plentiful (and so are mice, rats, and garden worms!).

If you want to find a fox,
you can look in the morning

or the afternoon—

but dawn and dusk are best.

Red foxes are busy both day and night, but your chances of sneaking a peek are better very early in the morning or at twilight, when they are hunting. Foxes eat a mixed menu of fruit, insects, birds, eggs, and small critters. And, unlike wolves or coyotes, foxes hunt on their own because what they catch is usually big enough for just one hungry belly.

You can look in the spring,

or the summer,

or the autumn . . .

or even the winter.

Foxes don't hibernate: they spend the whole year out and about. But a fox will look different depending on the season. That's because in the winter, red foxes have thick coats that keep them warm. By spring, this longer, heavier fur starts to fall out in clumps so that by summer, red foxes sport much sleeker haircuts.

But DON'T look in the sky,

or the trees,

or the river,

or the pond.

It's true that the gray wolf can climb trees, but you're more likely to find a red fox taking a nap or playing in tall grass. And while foxes are good swimmers, they don't have any need to be near water, other than if they're thirsty.

Do look for four fast feet,

amber eyes,

and a soft tail tipped in white.

Red foxes have black "socks" or fur on their legs, golden eyes with vertical pupils that help them see better at night, and fluffy tails called brushes. Their tails not only keep them warm when they curl in a snug circle, but they also help them balance as they zig and zag after prey.

Do look here,

and here,

and there.

Oops—just don't look when it's raining!

Foxes move into hidden dens (burrows that their neighbors such as rabbits and badgers have abandoned) during bad weather or to give birth and raise their babies—called pups, cubs, or kits—in spring. Pups stay with their parents through summer, learning important things like how to play and hunt. In autumn, they head out to start their own fox families.

Look for *these* tracks—

A single line of tracks is the trademark of a fox's trot. A fox puts her right back foot in the print of her front left foot and vice versa, leaving behind a neat and tidy trail.

not these . . .

or these.

Listen for yips,

yowls,

and growls.

Red foxes make a range of noises, though none of them sound much like a common dog's barking. Instead, foxes' high-pitched howls, chirps, and screams are more birdlike. . . . And sometimes, a fox can even sound like a person crying. Different calls are used when playing, or fighting, or when fox parents want to warn their babies of danger.

If you want to find a fox,
you must be as still as a pebble . . .

and as quiet as the moon.

You must be willing to wait . . .
and wait.

And if a fox finds YOU,
know that you are lucky indeed!

Foxes are wary and shy and want to avoid humans—and it's good for people
and wild animals to keep a respectful distance. But foxes can also be curious.
If you are patient, quiet, and still—just like the photographer of this book—you
might be rewarded with a glimpse of a graceful and fabulous fox!

A note from photographer
Ossi Saarinen

I've been in love with animals since I was a little kid. I always felt happy when I saw them in books or on nature shows on TV. For me, animals always seem energetic, smart, funny, and adorable. As I grew older, I started looking for animals in the forests near my home in Finland. I would watch them for hours and imagine what it would be like to be their friend.

When I saw wild foxes for the very first time, I was so excited to get a photo that I walked straight toward them, which, of course, made the foxes run away! Since then, I have learned how to approach wild animals. Calmness and silence are very important for a wildlife photographer. The second time I encountered foxes, I quietly lay on the forest floor for a couple hours one morning, only a few meters away from four adorable fox cubs. I ended up taking photos that I still consider some of the best I've ever taken. That day, I really fell in love with photographing wild animals.

Whenever I discover an animal in the wild, I must be very careful. Any sudden movement or sound may scare them away. If I remain quiet, calm, and respectful of their space, the animals become accustomed to seeing me and are not afraid.

I have had so much fun gaining the trust of these beautiful creatures and taking photographs of them. I hope that you enjoy the photos, too. And, who knows, maybe one day you will be lucky enough to find a fox!

To learn more about foxes:

London, Jonathan. *Little Fox in the Snow*. Somerville: Candlewick Press, 2018.

Markle, Sandra. *Foxes*. Minneapolis: Lerner Publications Company, 2010.

Pringle, Laurence. *The Secret Life of the Red Fox*. Honesdale: Boyds Mills Press, 2017.

Sebastian, Emily. *Foxes*. New York: The Rosen Publishing Group, Inc., 2012.

Thompson, Jolene. *Faraway Fox*. Boston: Houghton Mifflin Harcourt, 2016.